INSPIRED

A Collection of Poems for the Soul

JANET WU

ILLUSTRATED BY: SIERRA MON ANN VIDAL

To order additional copies of this book, contact:
Xlibris
844-714-8691
www.Xlibris.com
Orders@Xlibris.com

ISBN: Softcover   978-1-6641-8788-7
         EBook   978-1-6641-8789-4

Print information available on the last page

Rev. date: 08/03/2021

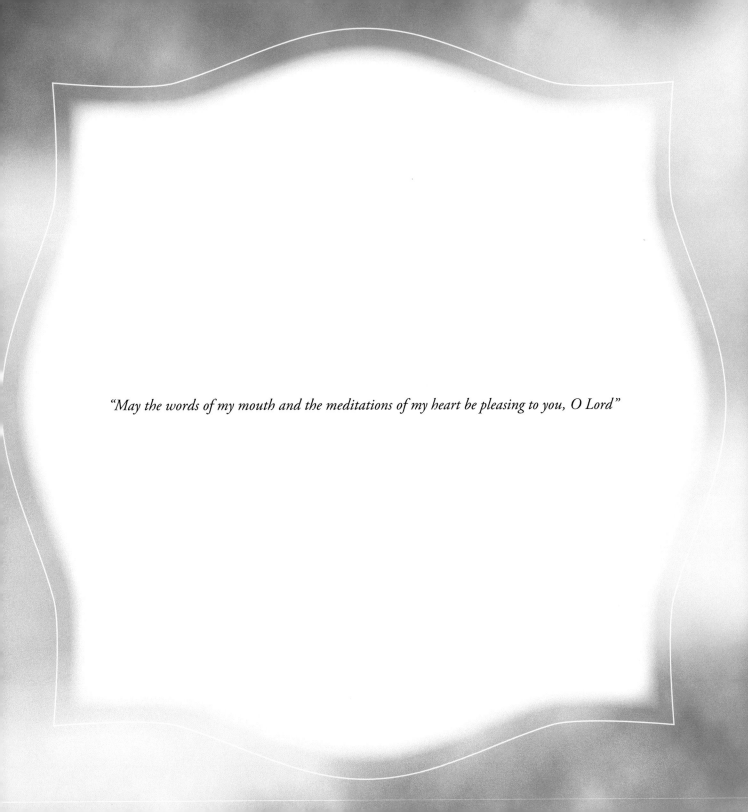

"May the words of my mouth and the meditations of my heart be pleasing to you, O Lord"

Contents

I.   Colorful Inspirations

III. Ideas and Things Inspiration

I.

COLORFUL INSPIRATIONS

Green
means go.
Red means
agape.
Orange is
Jesus Christ
the mediator
between law
and grace.

Yellow is signal for the coming Light.
Blue is divine protection in camouflage.
Purple is Christ's love with grace, mercy
and peace to all.

White is
God's glory
shining in all
radiance.
Black is truth
and justice
for all.
Pink is
blooming
love with the
Savior.
Apple Green
is New Life in
Christ Jesus.
Peach is
sweet
surrender to
the Lord.

Green

Vibrant. Renewing.
Safety guard
The most humble of all colors
It brings life, it shows the way
Leading into eternal divine grace
Safely home at last
I'm gonna stay
I'm gonna stay
Stay in this heavenly realm.

Red

Stop. Park.
Follow me, then you shall find
A place for rest
A place to park
I am the way to find you rest
Come with me, and you shall be
In a land of paradise
Forever be.

Orange

Young. Bold.
Bright. Invigorating.
I'm willing to try out
New experiences
Cutting across
All bordering edges.
With one heart and mind
Break down barriers, create new heights
In this new millennial age.
Heaven is cheering you on
To pursue fantastic new dreams
Seize the moment
Make it great
You'll find endless possibilities
When you reach your destination.

Yellow

Be cautious. Beware.
What lies ahead
Who knows what not
Lower the chin,
Bend your knees
Watch out for the coming light
That shows you the way
Never look back
Follow the signaling light.

Blue

Camouflage. Safety net.
The friendliest of all colors
Brings comfort, brings love
I feel like I am home at last
Hospital care
Escort buses
Police uniforms
All under the
Grace and protection
Of Heavenly Father's love and care.

Purple

Romantic. Elegant.
The most royal of all colors
It makes perfect sense to eat some eggplants.
Dignity is your character.
You are the most loving, the most caring
You let down your guards and show your true heart
Even when it's vulnerable.
I don't know why I love you so much
Because you are so divine.

White

Pure. Pristine.
The color of all colors
Yet so humble and modest
It takes away the imperfection of all other colors
By dabbing on the last
Perfecting touch.

Black

Mysterious. Concealed.
The color guard of all colors
"It's a mystery," they used to say
How foolish it is
Without asking the whys.
Just ask the black box
Then it will say
That the answers you seek and find
Are all inside.
Just ask me
Then I will answer
With the noblest of all truths.

Pink

Lovely. Romantic.
The most lovable of all colors
Signifies blooming love with the Savior.
Outpoured with hot-pink paint from head to toe
Overflowing with the Savior's love and grace
Need not be dismayed by the overwhelming love
Accept it and you shall find
That there are many others who are your kind.

Apple Green

Rebirth. Renewal.
It is the brand-new color of all colors.
You find newness and renewal in here
No one else exists, nothing else matters
Except you.
Rejuvenated and refreshed
Here is a chance for new beginning
To redefine and relive an entirely new you.

Peach

Sweet. Kind.
The sweetest of all colors.
It brings you great delight
As you unravel your deepest desires
It does not disappoint; it truly satisfies
Like a gracious mother that nurtures and nourishes
That makes you feel like the happiest babe on earth.
It surrenders all to the asking
Holding nothing back.
Fills the empty heart
That brings you back to wholesomeness
With a dash of sweet love.

II.

DIVINE AND PEOPLE INSPIRATIONS

Lord, You Set Me Free

Lord, you set my soul so free
Freely, you set my soul
Freely, I flow in your stream of mercy and kindness
Your grace is amazing to me.

You hear every cry I cry
You listen to every word in my heart
You answer every prayer I pray
You heal deep wounds in my soul.

I will bow down to you
I will bow down to you

You are a wonderful Maker
You are a wonderful Deliverer
You are a wonderful Savior.

A Devotion for Thee

Lord, you right me when I am wrong
You set me free when I'm in bondage
You rescue me when I'm in trouble
You give me hope when I'm disparaged
You answer me when I call
You lift me up when I'm down
You make a way when there seems no way
You are my healer my deliverer my provider
You are my all in all
My one and only true God

Sister

For a sister so wise, she has infinite understanding
And foresight into the unknown
For a sister so wise, she sees the deep end of things
And makes righteous judgment
For a sister so understanding, she comprehends the above and beyond
And dwells in safety and peace
She makes no rash decisions
But with love and understanding
She brings about a peaceful end to all things
She is my sister beloved
A mother of one and a wife to a man
And a sister to me

OS Professor Came to Town

My OS professor just came to town
And asked us to write some codes
She said first create a process called foo
Then set its pointer to infile
Next make another pointer and set it to outfile
Then the rest will take care of itself.
I said, "Is that all there is to it?"
To create and change the pointer?
And she said, yes, that's all there is to it
And I said, what about memory consideration?
She said
Why not just buy some more memories
And put them in the computer?
And I said
No, ma'am, what to do with floating and unused pointers?
Yes, darling, I understand
All you have to do is to create and set pointers
Unused pointers will be swept away.

Ideology and Reality

I have a friend who sat in a Queer English Literature class
She said
The professor lectured that
Different people in different professions
Wear different outfits.
Hospital doctors wear white lab coats
Court judges wear black toga robes
College professors wear suites or blouses.
Then a student in white T-shirt and blue jeans raised her hand up
And said
"But I am a professor too."

Feeling Like a Child

I feel like a child
Wanting to crave for more
I feel like a child
Wanting to create a perfect world
I feel like a child
Wanting to break the mortal laws
I feel like a child
As if I am made anew
Every day I wonder
What do I know?
Every night I ask
What don't I know?
I'm not going to care anymore
What I know and what don't I know
In the end, all it matters
Is the perfect love that I know.

For Him

No, you are not gay
Who told you that you are gay?
Every little thing that you do tells me that you are a man
A real man.

Every word that you said
Everything that you are
Tell me that you are a man
A real man.

Yes, you are a sensitive soul
Yes, sometimes you whine a little, cry a little
Shout a little and even nag a little
Like a big grown-up child
But that's you
That's just you.

Yes, you are a carefree soul
You say the stupidest thing
And yet sounds so profound
That amazes the crowd
But that's you
That's just you.

Yes, you may pretend a little in front of the insensible crowd
Acting a little tough, talking a little high up
Lest they see that the
Gentle and vulnerable spirit inside of you
And that's you
That's the real you

Yes, you may act like a child when no grown-ups are around
Making silly puns and saying nonsense stuff that no one laughs at but you
And that's you
That's just you
The innocent, carefree you.

No, you are not gay
Who told you that you are gay?
Every little thing about you tell me that you are a man
A real, mature man.

When your face wanes with sideburns
When your voice sounds deeper
When we were young, I eye witnessed
As you gave your first kiss
To that pretty girl in the garden
How your face blushed and smiled
And that's you
That's the real you.

Now that you are older
You may act a little feminine, a little queer
In the eyes of worldly souls
You never go along with the world
Doing things in your unique ways
Asking questions from the heart
That astounds the world
But that's you
That's just you
The real, free-spirited you.

Your pure and gentle words outpour
Like the purest thing more than the bluest sky
Giving me strength and hope
And nourish my body and soul.
So sweet and gentle
That comfort my feeble soul
And that's you
That's just you
The loving, sweet you.

How great and perceptive are your eyes
When the lights of our eyes met
By your sheer understanding of the light
You simply knew them all
And that's you
That's just you
The real you that I have known.

No, you are not gay
Who told you that you are gay?
Every little thing about you reveals that you are a true man.
Above all, God does not make mistakes
Moreover
I love you so.

III.

IDEAS AND THINGS INSPIRATION

Yogurt

Open the cap
Flip the cover
Take the big, fat spoon
And swirl it around
The white mixes with red
The red mixes with white
Slowly the pretty twirls
Become one homogeneous thing
Take a spoonful, and you shall find
That the flavor is indeed
Sweet and sour, like one

Poetry 101

First silence your thoughts
Then listen to the voice within
Pay attention to the things
And your words that tie to them
Stay close to the people who do what they say
And I guarantee you that
You shall find the art in you

A Rage to Master

Focus your mind on a single thought
Hold on to the thought then it fires
With madness it rages
With rage it thunders
A rage to master
To master the soul

No More

He turned around
Look down upon the corner
He saw something odd
I said don't do this again
He asked why not?
I said just don't
Because there is no more

Fading Glory

Watching the sun comes down
Behind the black greenery curtain
Second by second
The radiance fading away
Fraction by fraction
The round orange face sinks behind
Until the dimming light
Leaves a last shine
Saying goodbye
To the day's end

Hog Dog Eating Machine

Take a bite from the end
Chew it in the mouth
Let the hot, burning smell
Dwell in the hollow mouth.

Then squeeze a line of ketchup
Litter it all over
On the slender, fried, juicy meat.

Take another bite in the middle of the red thing
A big awesome satisfying bite
Tasting wholesome deliciousness
In that perpetual eating machine.

Printed in the United States
by Baker & Taylor Publisher Services